A Life God Rewards

GIRLS 90 DAY CHALLENGE

BRUCE WILKINSON
WITH MACK THOMAS
AND DANAE JACOBSON

MULTNOMAH KIDZ

A LIFE GOD REWARDS GIRLS 90–DAY CHALLENGE
published by Multnomah Publishers, Inc.

© 2002 by Exponential, Inc.

International Standard Book Number: 1-59052-099-8

Design and photography by Koechel Peterson & Associates, Inc., Minneapolis, MN

Italics in Scripture quotations are the author's emphasis.

Unless otherwise indicated, Scripture quotations are from:

The Holy Bible, New International Reader's Version,
Copyright © 1994, 1996 by International Bible Society.
Used by permission of Zondervan Publishing House.
All rights reserved.

Other Scripture quotations:
The Holy Bible, New Century Version (NCV)
© 1987, 1988, 1991 by Word Publishing
Used by permission.

Multnomah is a trademark of Multnomah Publishers, Inc.,
and is registered in the U.S. Patent and Trademark Office.

Printed in the United States of America

For information:

MULTNOMAH PUBLISHERS, INC.
POST OFFICE BOX 1720
SISTERS, OREGON 97759

02 03 04 05 06 07 08—10 9 8 7 6 5 4 3 2 1 0

Hey, girls,
here's an invitation you can't resist:

Come into the pages of this book, and change your life for the better…forever! That's exactly what will happen when you apply these awesome truths about God's rewards.

Here's the deal:

This book is divided into three 30-day sections. You may want to go through the first thirty, one per day, and then think about what you read for a few days before moving on to the next section. Or you can take the 90-day challenge with a friend or a small group and talk together about what you've read each day.

Whatever you decide, one thing is certain: Reading this book will be a rewarding experience!

May 2003

S	M	T	W	T	F	S
				1	2	3
4	5	6	7	8	9	10
11	12	13	14	15	16	17
18	19	20	21	22	23	24
25	26	27	28	29	30	31

June 2003

S	M	T	W	T	F	S
1	2	3	4	5	6	7
8	9	10	11	12	13	14
15	16	17	18	19	20	21
22	23	24	25	26	27	28
29	30					

July 2003

S	M	T	W	T	F	S
		1	2	3	4	5
6	7	8	9	10	11	12
13	14	15	16	17	18	19
20	21	22	23	24	25	26
27	28	29	30	31		

August 2003

S	M	T	W	T	F	S
					1	2
3	4	5	6	7	8	9
10	11	12	13	14	15	16
17	18	19	20	21	22	23
24	25	26	27	28	29	30
31						

PART ONE

God Wants to Reward You!

What exactly is the link between what you do today and what you will experience after you go to heaven?

Let God show you His answers to these questions and so much more. Come discover how your future is the key to unlocking the power of your today. Now you can live with the absolute certainty that everything you do today matters forever.

DAY 1

A Sure Promise

David once said:

*"The LORD rewards every man
for his righteousness and faithfulness."*
1 Samuel 26:23, NIV

Saul was chosen by God to be king of Israel, but like every person, he sometimes disobeyed God. Saul was searching for a young warrior, David, with plans to kill him. But one day, Saul was caught asleep, and David had the chance to kill Saul. Yet David chose not to kill the king because God did not want him to. David chose to obey God.

When Saul found out what had happened, he promised never to try to harm David again. Saul told him, "May the LORD reward you well for the way you treated me today" (1 Samuel 24:19, NIV). And when you obey God, He will reward you, too!

❀ Hold That Thought ❀

Pray and ask God to show you what He wants you to do with your day today. Then keep your eyes open for opportunities to obey God or do something nice for a family member, a friend, or a neighbor. God will show you how to earn His rewards if you ask Him.

DAY 2

The Best Exercise

Physical exercise has some value, but spiritual exercise is much more important, for it promises a reward in both this life and the next. This is true, and everyone should accept it.

1 Timothy 4:8–9

Margo is an amazing soccer player. Everywhere she goes, she always has a soccer ball with her. Margo practices all the time. Sometimes she plays with the kids who live next door, and sometimes she practices with her teammates. Other times she works on drills by herself at home.

There are lots of physical things you can do, too. Maybe you like rock climbing or skiing. Maybe you play baseball or run track. Maybe you like swimming or just walking around, exploring. It is important to stay active and healthy physically, but it's even more important to stay active and healthy spiritually. Talking to God, doing things for others, reading the Bible—these are all ways to stay spiritually healthy. So what do you think? Let's get healthy and stay healthy. Let's go!

❀ Hold That Thought ❀

Make time today for a good spiritual workout. Read your Bible, talk to God, and do something special for someone else. It could be as simple as washing the dishes for your mom or reading to your baby sister.

DAY 3

What Would Jesus Do?

As we know Jesus better, his divine power gives us everything we need for living a godly life.
2 Peter 1:3

A few years ago, jewelry, T-shirts, and caps sporting the letters WWJD were all the rage among Christian kids. The four letters—short for the question "What would Jesus do?"—remind us that everything we do or say should be modeled after how Jesus Himself lived here on earth.

But how can we really know what Jesus would do here and now? How would He react to today's popular music and movies? How would He deal with peer pressure at school or from kids in the neighborhood?

We can know exactly what Jesus would do by simply getting to know Him better. How? Jesus wants to teach us all about Himself! Listen to His voice. "Come to me," He says. "Let me teach you" (Matthew 11:28-29).

Come to Jesus today by praying and reading His Word, and let Him teach you all about Himself and what He would do in your shoes.

❀ Hold That Thought ❀

What do you want to know most about Jesus? Talk to Him today about what you admire most about Him. Praise Him for this. And ask Him to keep teaching you about Himself. By getting to know Jesus better and better, you can live the kind of life that God rewards.

✿ Hold That Thought ✿

Doing right in God's eyes means more than just making the right choices. It means letting Jesus be totally alive inside you, so that His life spills out in everything you do. Let Jesus be completely in charge of what you do today.

Doing Right

The LORD rewarded me for doing right.
Psalm 18:20

Sometimes it's really tough to do what you know is right. Have you ever been with a friend who wanted to watch a movie you weren't allowed to see or listen to music you knew was bad? What did you do?

Lisa and Jamie went to the movie theater one Saturday afternoon with Lisa's big sister. She bought them tickets for the new G-rated animated film. But once inside, Lisa and Jamie snuck into the screen showing a romantic thriller—a PG-13 movie that neither of their parents would allow them to see, but that everyone at school was talking about.

Jamie was feeling terribly guilty, even as the previews played. Before the movie started, Jamie stood up and told Lisa that her parents wouldn't want her to see this film and that she was going to watch the G-rated movie instead. Lisa laughed and made fun of Jamie in front of several classmates in the audience.

Lisa apologized the next day. She told Jamie that the movie hadn't been so good after all and that she was feeling pretty guilty about seeing it herself.

It's hard to do what is right, especially when your friends are doing something else. But when you choose to do what's right, God will reward you for it. Even if no one else realizes, God still sees and He will reward you. And that's a promise!

Time for You

Do not throw away this confident trust in the Lord, no matter what happens. Remember the great reward it brings you!
Hebrews 10:35

When Jesus was living on the earth, people wanted to talk to Him all the time. He was very busy, but guess what? When Jesus was around kids—kids just like you—He would stop what He was doing and talk to them, play with them, and even hold the younger ones on His lap. People told Him to ignore them, but to Jesus, kids were just as important as anyone else. He knew that they trusted Him, and He even told everyone that they should trust God and love Him in the same way kids did.

No matter what happens in your life, remember that Jesus always has time for you. Always. Keep trusting in Him, because He'll never leave you.

❀ Hold That Thought ❀

What are you trusting God to do in your life right now? What do you think He wants you to trust Him with? Are you having trouble in school? Do you have a friend who needs His help? Maybe your mom or dad is sick. What can you do? Tell God and trust Him.

What Kind of Gardener Will You Be?

He who sows righteousness reaps a sure reward.
Proverbs 11:18, NIV

You know what happens when you plant seeds? If you plant an apple seed, an apple tree grows—not a tomato vine or a cactus. If you plant enough grass seed, a lawn will spring up, not a field of corn or a flower bed.

Becky and her younger brother Tommy decided they wanted to plant a garden. Their mom gave them some seeds, although she didn't remember what they were. The next morning, Tommy and Becky worked hard and planted every single seed. Every day, Becky and Tommy took turns watering the patch of dirt. And each day they found that nothing had changed, until one morning on Becky's watering day, she saw a few tiny green sprouts.

"All right!" she said. "Now we can finally figure out what these seeds will grow into." A couple of weeks later, a healthy crop of carrots was growing in the ground.

Whatever kinds of seeds you plant each day of your life—bad seeds or good seeds, seeds of foolishness or seeds of righteousness—will decide what you're going to get later on. What kinds of seeds are you going to plant today?

❧ Hold That Thought ❧

If you will do good things today—that's what planting seeds of righteousness means—the seeds will grow into a golden crop of heavenly rewards.

DAY 7

Seeds of Peace

God promises:

*Those who are peacemakers will plant seeds of peace
and reap a harvest of goodness.*

James 3:18

You have decided to be a good gardener. Today you are going to plant peace. How will you do this? Well, instead of heading out to plant seeds in the dirt, you go to school. Before class, you hear two girls fighting about who their best friend is. Gently, you remind them that all friends are special and it's not something to fight about. You've just planted a seed of peace.

At lunchtime, one of the older boys tries to take a younger boy's lunch because he forgot his own. Quickly you offer to share some of your lunch with the older boy. You've just planted a seed of peace.

That night at dinner, when your mom asks you to clear the table, you say yes with a happy heart. You've just planted a seed of peace.

As you go to sleep, you quietly pray for your friend who doesn't know Jesus. You've just planted a seed of peace.

❀ Hold That Thought ❀

All day, every day, we plant seeds. What kind of seeds you choose to plant is up to you. Ask God to show you how you can plant seeds of peace today. Then keep your eyes open and watch for every opportunity to plant seeds for God.

DAY 8

Totally Committed

This is why Jesus died:

He gave his life… to make us his very own people,
totally committed to doing what is right.

Titus 2:14

Have you ever watched the Olympic games? Everybody who competes in the Olympics has to be extremely good at what they do. Most of the athletes train every single day. Many of them work out for longer than you are in school each day! Each competitor has to be completely committed to her sport, or she won't have a chance at winning a medal.

Each of us has a choice: whether or not to live all day, every day, for Jesus. Remember that someone died so that we could live. That someone is Jesus. So what do you say? Are you up for this? Committing your life to Jesus is a lot of hard work, but in the end it's worth much more than an Olympic gold medal.

❧ Hold That Thought ❧

God never sleeps. He never dozes off. His Spirit is at work all the time with explosive, dynamic energy. And He makes His Spirit available to you! Ask the Holy Spirit to give you the strength to be committed.

The Power of Words

*From the fruit of his lips a man is filled with good things
as surely as the work of his hands rewards him.*

Proverbs 12:14, NIV

Kristin was sitting with a group of friends at lunchtime. They started saying really mean things about a girl named Jane who was at another table. At first, Kristin didn't say anything. But when she did, her friends were surprised at what she had to say. Kristin began pointing out some good things about Jane.

Jane may never know how Kristin stuck up for her, but it doesn't matter. Kristin will be rewarded for the good things that came out of her mouth. Also, by saying good things about Jane, Kristin influenced the rest of the group. They stopped tearing Jane down, and some of them even became friends with her.

Words are powerful things. They can bring about so much good, but they also can do a lot of harm. What kinds of words are coming out of your mouth?

❀ Hold That Thought ❀

What kinds of things have you said that were harmful instead of helpful? Maybe you talked back to your mom or snapped at your sister. Ask God to forgive you for that. Now think of five people you're likely to talk to in the next twenty-four hours. What can you say to each one that will encourage that person?

Stop and Ask for Directions

Be ready to do whatever is good.
Titus 3:1, NIV

As Mrs. James handed out the math test, Zach immediately started working on his. He didn't bother reading the directions. The rest of the class was still working when Zach turned in his test to Mrs. James.

A couple of days later, Zach got his test back. There were red marks all over it and a big F at the top. Mrs. James called Zach up to her desk after class. "Zach," she said, "if you had read the directions, I know you would have done great on this test."

Just as Zach was given directions with his math test, God has given us directions for life. The Bible is our guidebook that teaches us how to live our lives for God. But it's up to you to read it. Are you going to charge ahead like Zach? Or will you take time to read the directions?

❧ Hold That Thought ❧

Do you sometimes feel a little lost, like when you're not sure how to act or what to say in a certain situation? Well, now you can be prepared for anything! Start every day by reading from God's manual for life.

What a Friend!

*As we know Jesus better, his divine power gives us
everything we need for living a godly life.*
2 Peter 1:3

How do you get to know Jesus better? Well, how do you get to know your friends better? By hanging out with them and talking with them, right? You would never get to know anyone if you didn't spend time with them, would you? It's the same way with Jesus. We can only get to know Him by spending time with Him—talking to Him, listening to Him, and reading His words.

Isn't it kind of cool to know that you have a friend who is always there with you, no matter what? He wants you to get to know Him more. So talk to Him, love Him, hang out with Him. He's there, and He's the best friend you could ever ask for!

❀ Hold That Thought ❀

Think of your closest friends. What kinds of things do you do together? Jesus wants to be that kind of friend to you. He wants to be your very best friend. And He wants to go everywhere with you. Talk to Him. Tell Him what you have planned for the day, and invite Him to come along!

Little Things

Jesus said:

"If you give even a cup of cold water to one of the least of my followers, you will surely be rewarded."

Matthew 10:42

Bring a cold cup of water when someone is thirsty. Give a hug to show you care. Offer a flower to make someone smile. Just for doing these simple things, Jesus says that "you will surely be rewarded."

The little things matter to Jesus. What else can you do for someone today? Maybe you can help Mom prepare dinner or do your chores without being asked. Smile at a friend who looks sad, or do something for a neighbor who is sick. It doesn't matter if it's big or small, Jesus sees and it makes Him happy! And He will reward you.

❀ Hold That Thought ❀

Today, remember this thought: Little things on earth mean a lot in heaven.

DAY 13

A Friend in Need

When God's children are in need, be the one to help them out.
Romans 12:13

Morgan's mom had told her to hurry home right after school. They were going shopping together, and she wanted to get back home in plenty of time for dinner. So as soon as the bell rang, Morgan jumped up, grabbed her backpack, and raced to the parking lot. On her way to the car, she heard a noise. She stopped because it sounded like someone was crying. Morgan looked around and saw a young girl crouched in the corner, her head buried between her knees. *I have to go,* thought Morgan. *I don't have time to stop and talk to this girl.* But Morgan wanted to make sure the girl was okay.

Morgan walked over and the girl looked up, tears streaming down her face. "Are you okay?" Morgan asked.

The girl wiped her face with her sleeve. "I'm just really sad because my dad is in the hospital right now. And I'm scared and worried about him." Right then, Morgan knew she had made the right choice—to stop and show concern. Shopping, she decided, could wait a few more minutes. This girl needed her right now, just to talk to.

Sometimes it's hard to help those in need, especially when we have things of our own to do. But remember, Jesus gave His entire life for us. You can give a little bit of your life to help others. It will always be worth it.

❀ Hold That Thought ❀

Jesus helps you with your needs so that you can help others with theirs. See what you can do today to bring love and comfort to others.

DAY 14

Working for Jesus

Work hard and cheerfully at whatever you do,
as though you were working for the Lord rather than for people.
Remember that the Lord will give you an inheritance as your reward,
and the Master you are serving is Christ.

Colossians 3:23–24

There are six kids in the MacDonald family. Both of the parents work, and they still don't have very much money. That means that all of the kids, especially the oldest two, have to help out a lot. They watch their younger brothers and sisters, keep the house clean, and sometimes even make dinner. You probably help with dinner every once in a while or pitch in with housecleaning if your parents ask, but for the MacDonald kids, this is everyday life. The older kids don't get to play with friends very often because they are busy helping out at home.

Do you know what the amazing thing is? They don't complain about the work! They are always happy to help because they know that they are really doing it for Jesus.

Have you ever thought about that? God says that He will reward those who work hard and cheerfully for Him. It doesn't matter what you're doing. You could be emptying the dishwasher, doing your homework, or mowing someone's lawn. Whatever it is, you can do it for Jesus!

❀ Hold That Thought ❀

What does "working for the Lord" mean to you? What difference does it make in how you study or work? Think about it today as you do your homework or chores.

Loving Every Moment

Moses taught us to pray this prayer:

Teach us to make the most of our time, so that we may grow in wisdom.
Psalm 90:12

When Kayla was born, the doctors told her parents that she was weak and would probably only live to about age twelve. Growing up, Kayla considered every minute to be a gift from God. When Kayla's little brother was born, she would hold him for hours because she knew she might not get to hold him or play with him later on. When Kayla and her family went to Disneyland, she enjoyed every minute of it because she wasn't sure she would ever get to go back. Whenever she had a chance to tell someone how much Jesus loved them, she always did because she knew she might not have another chance. Whenever she said good-bye to someone, she always told them she loved them because she didn't know if she would see them again.

Kayla lived her life the way all of us should. She cherished every moment, every second. She died when she was twelve, but you know what? She was ready. She made the most of the time she had, and she didn't have any regrets.

❀ Hold That Thought ❀

Are you making the most of every hour of every day? Do you take every opportunity to do something good? Are you sharing God's love with others when you get the chance? Think about it. What will you do with today?

DAY 16

This Little Light of Mine

You are light in the Lord. Walk as children of light.
Ephesians 5:8, NKJV

For some reason, basements are always dark and scary at night. (Some of them are scary during the daytime, too!) When Abby was growing up, she hated going down to the basement by herself. It was so dark and it smelled funny. Sometimes she heard noises, but she could never tell if there was really something there or if it was just her imagination. What Abby discovered, though, was that the tiniest flashlight or candle would light up the whole basement. The darkness seemed to scurry away, and her fear would vanish with it.

In the Bible, God tells us to "walk as children of light." We are flashlights and candles in a dark and sometimes scary world. Darkness can't survive where there is light. So how can you let your light shine in your world today?

❀ Hold That Thought ❀

Are you ever afraid of the dark? What about when you see the dark and evil things in the world around you? Guess what? With Jesus, you don't need to be afraid of anything! When you let His light shine through you, the darkness will disappear and you can show others the way to Him. Pray and ask God to show you how you can be Jesus' shining light in your family, in your school, and everywhere you go.

Small Sacrifice, Big Reward

And do not forget to do good and to share with others,
for with such sacrifices God is pleased.
Hebrews 13:16, NIV

Cammy and Nicole were sisters, close in age and almost the same size. Sometimes they would wear each other's clothes, but the rule was that they didn't wear each other's new clothes. One day Nicole was getting ready for her piano recital when she saw the cute new dress Cammy had been given for her birthday. Nicole knew the rule about new clothes but asked Cammy if she could borrow the dress. At first it was really hard for Cammy, but in her heart she knew Nicole would look great in it and that the recital was important to her sister. So even though the dress was brand-new and she'd never worn it herself, Cammy let Nicole wear it.

When we do good things like share our money and possessions with others (even when it is hard for us to do), God is pleased. And when we please God, He will be sure to reward us in heaven.

❁ Hold That Thought ❁

What do you have that you can share today with someone who truly needs it? Ask God to help you share with a joyful heart.

Praising Jesus!

Through Jesus, therefore, let us continually offer to God a sacrifice of praise.
Hebrews 13:15, NIV

Have you ever done something for someone else when it meant you had to give up something you wanted to do? Have you ever picked up around the living room, even though it wasn't your mess, because you knew your mom liked to keep a clean house? Have you ever raked the lawn so that it would be easier for your dad to mow?

Those kinds of things are called "sacrifices." Another kind of sacrifice that makes God happy is when we praise Him with our mouths. Sometimes that means singing, saying encouraging things to other people, or just talking to God. He loves it when you praise Him, and He never gets tired of hearing your praise. So keep on praising Him with all your heart!

❀ Hold That Thought ❀

Praise that makes God happy is praise that comes through Jesus. Spend some time alone today just worshiping God. Think about all that Jesus has done for you. He died so that you can call God your Father. He died so you can go to heaven and live with Him forever and receive His rewards. Thank Him and praise Him!

DAY 19

A Cheerful Giver

God loves a cheerful giver.
2 Corinthians 9:7, NIV

Ryan and Tucker worked hard all week, earning money by shoveling snow for neighbors. The boys were saving money to buy new skateboards come spring. On their way to check out skateboards at the store, they saw a little girl with no coat, wearing tennis shoes full of holes. "Hey, little girl, where's your coat?" they called out.

"I don't have one," she said, her teeth chattering.

The boys looked at each other, and both thought of the money they had just earned. Ryan and Tucker walked with the girl to a store where they spent all their money on a coat, boots, hat, and gloves for the little girl. The boys were surprised by how much fun they had picking out and buying the gifts. Ryan and Tucker were what the Bible calls "cheerful givers." They gave happily and freely, and God loves it when we give like that.

❀ Hold That Thought ❀

When you give your money or time to help others, do you give cheerfully? Do you keep a pleasant attitude when you help your mom and dad around the house? Ask God to give you opportunities to help people in need. And ask Him to help you give with a cheerful heart.

Enemies or Friends?

Jesus said:

*"Love your enemies. Do good to those who hate you.
Pray for the happiness of those who curse you.
Pray for those who hurt you."*

Luke 6:27–28

Do you have enemies? I'm not talking about the kind you fight on a battlefield. What about a person you always argue with? Or maybe someone who did something really mean to you and whom you haven't forgiven? What about someone you are jealous of or someone you just don't like? There are all kinds of enemies. Guess how Jesus wants us to treat our enemies? He tells us to do good to them and to pray that they are happy, even when they are mean and hurt us! That sounds like how we should treat our friends, doesn't it? It might be easier if we start thinking of them as friends, rather than as enemies. Jesus is looking forward to rewarding us for loving others like He does!

❧ Hold That Thought ❧

God will reward you for loving someone who may not even like you. Next time someone puts you down or tries to pick a fight with you, be prepared to say a kind word to him or her in return. You may someday end up being friends!

DAY 21

True Friends

If your enemies are hungry, give them food to eat.
If they are thirsty, give them water to drink...
and the LORD will reward you.

Proverbs 25:21–22

I heard a story about a sweet girl named Brianna. Brianna was an only child; her mother died when she was just two years old, so Brianna was raised by her father. None of her clothes were very nice or stylish, but it didn't seem to bother her. The kids at school would sometimes tell her she had ugly clothes, but instead of getting mad and saying mean things in return, she was always kind. She treated everyone like a friend, even when they were cruel to her. For a long time, the kids continued to taunt her. Then one day, one of the meanest of the girls walked up to Brianna with tears in her eyes. She apologized and said that every time she had said something cruel and Brianna responded kindly, she knew she was wrong. Then she asked Brianna to forgive her. Brianna said, "I already have."

How do you respond when people are mean to you? Do you treat them like Brianna did, as a friend?

❁ Hold That Thought ❁

It's hard to show kindness to someone who treats you badly. But Jesus can help you. Ask Him now to help you respond to your enemies in a way that will please Him.

DAY 22

Okay to Be Different

David knew:

The LORD will fulfill his purpose for me.
Psalm 138:8, NIV

Kirk was different from most boys his age. He didn't play basketball or football. He didn't skateboard or snowboard. And he hated running. For a long time, Kirk was sad because he thought there must be something wrong with him. Why wasn't he good at sports like his friends? He didn't even enjoy playing sports at all. *What is wrong with me?* he wondered.

At church one Sunday a man played a song that he had written, and it was beautiful. Then the man told the congregation that God created every person to be different and to do different things. If everyone were the same, he said, the world would be a very boring place.

That day, Kirk went home and wrote some song lyrics of his own. He didn't know exactly what he was good at or what he really wanted to do with his life, but he knew that it was okay to be different. It was okay not to like sports. It was okay not to be athletic. He realized that God had created him the way he was for a reason, and that God had a plan and a purpose for him.

The same is true for you! As you go through the day, remember this: God had a special purpose in mind when He created you.

❀ Hold That Thought ❀

Do you sometimes feel like you're different from everyone around you? Well, God does have a unique purpose for you, and He has given you special gifts to fulfill your purpose. Ask God today to show you what He has planned for you, and ask Him to help you use your gifts to honor Him.

DAY 23

Just between Me and God

The Bible tells us this about Jesus:

He went up on a mountainside by himself to pray.
When evening came, he was there alone.

Matthew 14:23, NIV

A young girl named Shanna was camping with her family. She had brought along her favorite toy—a small plastic elephant. On the first day, Shanna found that her prized elephant was missing. Her parents told her that it was too small to find and that she had probably dropped it in the lake. "But God could help me find it, right?" she asked.

"Yes," her father said. "Just don't get your hopes up."

For the remainder of the trip, Shanna hid behind a large tree for several minutes a couple of times each day. There she prayed that God would help her to find her elephant. A few days later, as the family was packing up to leave, they heard a loud shriek. Shanna came running, clutching her little elephant. It had tooth marks in it, as if from an animal. Shanna knew it must have been on quite a journey to get back to her.

"All your searching paid off," her mom said. But Shanna just smiled, because she knew this was an answer to prayer—just between her and God.

✿ Hold That Thought ✿

God wants us to pray and believe He is going to answer. He likes it when we pray with other people who believe in Him. But He doesn't want us to brag about how much we pray or read the Bible. Pray in secret and God will openly reward you.

❀ Hold That Thought ❀

Sometimes you will think it's hard to obey God. Like telling the truth when it seems easier to tell a lie, or doing your chores when your friend asks you to play instead. But obedience to God earns rewards, both here on earth and in heaven. Thank God for His rewards, and pray that He will help you to obey Him.

DAY 24

Thunder, Lightning, and Obedience

The commandments of the LORD are right....
The laws of the LORD are true....
There is great reward for those who obey them.

Psalm 19:8–11

Madeline and Kevin were next-door neighbors. During the summer they often played outside together, building forts, playing catch, exploring, swimming, or whatever they thought of to do that day. But their moms had one strict rule: Madeline and Kevin must be home before the sun went down. One day, Madeline and Kevin discovered a cave out in the woods. They explored it all day until they saw that the sun was almost down. Even though they really wanted to keep exploring, they chose to obey and ran home.

Shortly after they got home a huge thunder and lightning storm blew into the neighborhood and shook both their houses. The next morning, Madeline and Kevin raced to the cave, only to find that it had collapsed during the storm. They suddenly realized that if they had not obeyed and gone home when they did, they might have been trapped in the cave when it collapsed. Suddenly their moms' rule didn't seem too strict.

Like Madeline's and Kevin's moms' rule, God's commands are given to us for a reason. They show us His love and protection. And God promises great rewards for those who obey Him.

DAY 25

Really Loving

Don't just pretend that you love others. Really love them.
Romans 12:9

Haley's Grandma Marie is very old. She needs help to do a lot of the things that you and I do every day without help. Haley visits her grandma every week. Sometimes they just sit and talk. Sometimes they watch a movie. Sometimes Haley reads a book to her grandma. Nurses come in to help Grandma Marie eat, get dressed, and even go to the bathroom. But it doesn't bother Haley. Now, Haley doesn't have to visit her grandma; she does it because she loves her and wants to spend time with her. Haley doesn't care that Grandma Marie can't feed herself anymore or clean up after herself. Haley isn't pretending to love her grandma just to be nice—she really loves her. That is the kind of love that God has for us and wants us to have for others. Do you truly love people, or do you sometimes pretend?

❀ Hold That Thought ❀

How can you truly show your love to someone today? Give your dad a big hug when he comes home from work? Help a friend with her chores? Call your grandma just to talk to her? Thank God for His love today, and ask Him to help you share it with others.

DAY 26

Your Choice to Make

This is what Moses did:

*He chose to share the oppression of God's people
instead of enjoying the fleeting pleasures of sin.
He thought it was better to suffer for the sake
of the Messiah than to own the treasures of Egypt,
for he was looking ahead to the great reward
that God would give him.*

Hebrews 11:25–26

One summer at camp, Scott decided to believe in Jesus and give his life to Him. But some of his friends at home made fun of people who loved Jesus, so he was worried about telling them about his decision. Scott thought about this for a long time and finally decided that he could not pretend he didn't love Jesus. Rather than trying to hide it, Scott knew that he had to tell his friends about Jesus, even if it meant being made fun of.

Scott made a choice that each of us has to make, and he made the one that will bring great rewards someday. Each of us has to decide whether we care more about God and what He thinks or about our friends and what they think. What is your choice?

✿ Hold That Thought ✿

Choose to live for Jesus today and every day. No matter what anyone says, remember that He will reward you for living for Him.

Where Does Your Help Come From?

God makes this promise to His people:

*"I will strengthen you. I will help you.
I will uphold you with my victorious right hand."*

Isaiah 41:10

Stewart and Laura decided that they were going to raise money for children who didn't have parents. Neither of them were old enough to have a job, so they weren't sure where to start. All they knew was that they wanted to help people. Their parents suggested that they pray and ask God to help. So every night after dinner, Stewart and Laura met on Laura's front porch and prayed.

A couple of weeks later, they started calling and asking friends and family members for ideas about how to raise money. Soon they had plenty of ideas, and several people made contributions of their own. Before long, what had started as just a thought grew into an exciting project to help others.

God tells us to look to Him for our help, because He wants to help us. Where do you look when you need help?

❀ Hold That Thought ❀

What do you need help with today? Working out a misunderstanding with a friend? Understanding your math homework? Being kind to your family? Ask God and He will help and strengthen you.

A Lifetime of Love

Our great desire is that you will keep right on loving others as long as life lasts, in order to make certain that what you hope for will come true.

Hebrews 6:11

Have you ever heard of a couple celebrating their golden wedding anniversary? That means they have been married for fifty years! Fifty years is half a century. They would have been married while as many as twelve different American presidents had served in the White House. They would have celebrated fifty Christmas mornings together and most likely raised a few children, too! That is love that lasts!

God wants you to have that kind of love for Him and for other people. He wants you to love Him with all your heart until you die. If you do, the Bible says you can be sure of the rewards that await you in heaven. After all, Jesus said the two greatest commandments are to love God and love others.

❀ Hold That Thought ❀

Ask God today to fill your heart to overflowing with love for Him and for others all day long.

DAY 29

Good Examples

Look at those who are honest and good,
for a wonderful future lies before those who love peace.

Psalm 37:37

Who do you think of when you hear the words honest, good, and peace loving? Your parents? Your pastor? A friend? God tells us to look at those people and to learn from them because a "wonderful future" is ahead of them. A wonderful future awaits you, too, as you learn to follow their examples. But don't forget: The best example we can ever follow is Jesus Himself.

❀ Hold That Thought ❀

Think of someone you know who seems especially honest. Think of someone you know who seems especially good. Now think of someone you know who seems especially peace loving. What can you learn from these people?

What's Important?

Remember that the Lord will reward
each one of us for the good we do.
Ephesians 6:8

Logan loved to help his dad work outside, whether it was mowing the lawn, cleaning the garage, or pumping up bike tires. Logan would grab whatever his dad needed and run messages between his dad and mom. Sometimes, Logan's dad would take him out for ice cream after they finished working. Logan looked forward to that, but even if he didn't get ice cream, he would still have helped his dad. He just wanted to be with him—that was the most important part to Logan.

Like Logan, we will be rewarded for the good we do—the Bible makes that clear. But in the end, isn't being with God the real reason we live for God? It's not the ice cream or the rewards. It is truly about loving and knowing Him.

❧ Hold That Thought ❧

Spend some time with God today. He will spend every day with you if you'll let Him! Ask Him each day what He wants you to do for Him. Thank Him for the rewards He has planned for you.

May 2003

S	M	T	W	T	F	S
				1	2	3
4	5	6	7	8	9	10
11	12	13	14	15	16	17
18	19	20	21	22	23	24
25	26	27	28	29	30	31

June 2003

S	M	T	W	T	F	S
1	2	3	4	5	6	7
8	9	10	11	12	13	14
15	16	17	18	19	20	21
22	23	24	25	26	27	28
29	30					

July 2003

S	M	T	W	T	F	S
		1	2	3	4	5
6	7	8	9	10	11	12
13	14	15	16	17	18	19
20	21	22	23	24	25	26
27	28	29	30	31		

August 2003

S	M	T	W	T	F	S
					1	2
3	4	5	6	7	8	9
10	11	12	13	14	15	16
17	18	19	20	21	22	23
24	25	26	27	28	29	30
31						

PART TWO

PART II

How God Will Reward You

What are the rewards that God wants to give you? What does the Bible say about His rewards and what you can do to earn them?

Let God show you His answers to these questions. Come discover how wonderful these rewards will be—all because of the overwhelming goodness of God.

A Prophet's Reward

Jesus said this:

*"If you welcome a prophet as one who speaks for God,
you will receive the same reward a prophet gets.
And if you welcome good and godly people
because of their godliness,
you will be given a reward like theirs."*

Matthew 10:41

One cool thing about God is that He is a promise keeper. He never, ever breaks His promises. One of His promises to us has to do with the prophets you read about in the Bible, like Daniel, Elijah, and John the Baptist. These were men who spoke for God. They spoke with God's authority. And because of this, people didn't always want to hear what the prophets had to say. They were often angry at God's prophets. But Jesus promised that those who welcomed the prophets of God would receive the same rewards in heaven that the prophets themselves would receive!

Jesus makes the same promise about how we treat men and women of God today. You probably feel like I do sometimes—that you don't deserve to receive the same rewards as some of the really good people we know who truly love God with all their hearts—but that's just what God promises. So be sure to show honor and respect to people whom you know have given their lives completely to God, and you will be given a reward like theirs.

☺ Hold That Thought ☺

Think of someone you know who is a "good and godly" person. Maybe it's the pastor of your church or the elderly lady on your block who used to teach Sunday school. Maybe it's even a girl at school who has been ridiculed by the other kids for her faith in God. Ask God to show you how you can honor that person today.

Who are the followers of Jesus that you respect and admire most? Your dad? Your pastor? Your teacher? Ask God to show you how you can serve them. By welcoming good and godly people like these and helping them, you will receive a reward like theirs.

Matching Rewards

Jesus said:

"If you welcome good and godly people because of their godliness, you will be given a reward like theirs."

Matthew 10:41

An elderly couple wanted the children in their town to know what true love is, so they held a contest. "Whoever can show us what true love is will win this brand-new bike," they announced. One boy knew that his little sister, Amber, really wanted to win, so he got his friends to help her. The boy and his friends were so busy helping Amber that they didn't even get to work on their own examples of true love.

The day of the contest arrived, and the town's kids brought everything imaginable to represent true love. One little boy brought his parents' wedding picture. One girl brought a CD player and played a pretty love song.

Amber had made a huge heart with names written inside and pictures glued onto it. She told the elderly couple how her brother and his friends had not finished their projects and helped her instead. The couple examined every child's example of true love, and then made their decision. "The bike goes to the little boy who gave up his own chance to win to help his sister. His friends will also each get a bike, because even though it wasn't their idea, they chose to help their friend."

Wow! The boys gave up their chances of winning to help someone else, and they also received prizes. That's what Jesus promises us, too. Can you believe it?

Hope That Makes You Smile

A prayer for you:

May the God of hope fill you with all joy and peace as you trust in him, so that you may overflow with hope by the power of the Holy Spirit.

Romans 15:13, NIV

I once heard about a boy named Kyle, and I pray that I can someday live like he did. Kyle was always smiling and laughing. He loved spending time with his family and playing with his friends. But most of all, Kyle loved Jesus. You see, Kyle was very sick and spent most of his time at the hospital or at home in bed. Time with his family was spent playing games, singing, watching movies—anything that could be done from bed.

"Playing with friends" meant doing whatever the boys could think of that Kyle could participate in without getting out of bed. Even though he couldn't do things like shoot a basketball, jump on a trampoline, or ride a horse, Kyle was happy with his life.

Sure, he wanted to do all those things, but he knew that God is a God of hope. He trusted that Jesus loved him and because of that, he had hope. Maybe he would never be healed on earth, but Kyle had the hope of heaven. You could see it in his eyes, in his smile, in his whole life! And guess what? You can have that hope, too! Jesus has made a way, and His rewards await us in heaven. We have so much to look forward to!

☙ Hold That Thought ☙

What are you looking forward to? Your birthday? A vacation? Being a teenager? Or maybe you don't feel like there's much to look forward to because of a less-than-perfect situation in your life. That's when it's good to think about all you have to look forward to in heaven. Thinking about the hope of heaven and the awesome rewards waiting for you there should give you a great start! God wants us to keep looking forward in hope.

DAY 4

Even When It's Tough

Make these words your own:

"I will trust God for my reward."
Isaiah 49:4

The day was scorching—almost 100 degrees—and playing softball was the last thing most people wanted to do. But this game was for the school championship, so the two teams were excited about playing. Sarah had been looking forward to this game all season. *I know we are going to win,* she thought to herself, *and I can't wait for Mom to take me shopping after the game.* Her mom had told her that when the season was over, she would buy Sarah a new mitt.

The other team scored right away. Then Sarah's team batted, and nobody even got past second base. By the sixth inning, Sarah's team was behind 11-3. By the end of the game, Sarah was roasting from the sun; but what bothered her more was that her team had lost.

Sarah's little brother bounded up and asked if she would still get a mitt, even though her team had lost. Although she was tired and frustrated, Sarah trusted what her mom had told her. "Yes," she said. "Mom promised me and I believe her."

☙ Hold That Thought ❧

What is the biggest discouragement or toughest situation that you're facing right now? Talk to God about it and ask for His help. No matter how hard things get, continue to trust in God.

God is like that. He can be trusted. So even when life is hard and you're upset or tired, remember that God is faithful. You can trust Him more than you can trust anyone else!

DAY 5

Treasure Trove

David praised God like this:

Your goodness is so great!
You have stored up great blessings
for those who honor you.

Psalm 31:19

Sometimes when people die, they leave all their money and possessions to close friends and relatives. In a small town called Kent, there was an old man named George. He had no family and very few friends. His clothes were old and sometimes smelled a little funny. George walked everywhere, so everybody in town assumed that he couldn't afford to buy a car. He spent a lot of time at the park, watching the kids swing and run around.

One day a boy named Samuel walked up to the bench where George was sitting and sat down beside him. From that time on Samuel talked to George whenever he saw him at the park. Slowly, Samuel and George became friends. Then one day Samuel heard that George had died. A few days later Samuel received a letter telling him that George had left a large sum of money for him. Unbeknownst to anyone in town, George had been storing up money all his life.

Did you know that God has stored up blessings for everyone who honors Him? Don't you want to be one of those people?

☙ Hold That Thought ❧

What have you done this week to honor God? You may have smiled at a stranger or helped your brother with his chores. Ask God to show you ways you can honor Him, so that you can receive the blessings He has stored up for you.

DAY 6

Scavenger Hunt

Jesus said this:

"Store up for yourselves treasures in heaven, where moth and rust do not destroy, and where thieves do not break in and steal. For where your treasure is, there your heart will be also."

Matthew 6:20–21, NIV

Have you ever been on a scavenger hunt? It's a game where everyone is given a list of unusual things to find. Then everyone splits up to see who can find the most items on the list. In the end, the person who gathers the most stuff wins.

As fun as scavenger hunts are, that's not how it works with God. God wants us to have treasure—valuable, everlasting treasure—but we don't get it by collecting stuff. The bumper sticker that says "The One Who Dies with the Most Toys Wins" may be funny, but it's not true. Real treasure is stored up in heaven.

To store treasure in heaven for yourself, you have to give here on earth. You love people and help them. You love God. True treasure isn't about getting; it's about giving.

Think about how you live. Are you on a scavenger hunt? Or are you storing up treasure and riches in heaven where they will last forever?

☽ Hold That Thought ☾

It's hard to imagine what God's rewards will be like. But Jesus tells us that by sharing what we have with others today, we are storing up treasures that we will be able to enjoy forever. Thank Jesus today for helping you to share with others, and tell Him how excited you are to see the treasures He has waiting for you.

DAY 7

God Pleasers

While we live, we live to please the Lord.
Romans 14:8

Have you ever heard of "people pleasers"? People pleasers try to do just that—please people. But they often get carried away. They make all their decisions based on what someone else wants them to do. People pleasers worry so much about making everyone around them happy, they forget that God is who they need to live for. Although He wants us to help others, God is who we should be trying to please.

So what kind of person are you going to be—a people pleaser or a God pleaser?

☉ Hold That Thought ☉

When you help others, are you doing it to make them like you? Or are you helping others because it pleases God? The Bible tells us, "Whether you eat or drink or whatever you do, do it all for the glory of God" (1 Corinthians 10:31, NIV). Think about why you are doing the things you do today.

DAY 8

A Secret Surprise

Jesus said this:

"Give your gifts in secret, and your Father, who knows all secrets, will reward you."

Matthew 6:4

Elizabeth woke up early one summer morning. She went outside and picked a bunch of wildflowers still glistening with dew. She put the colorful bouquet in a jar and set it on the front porch of the neighbor girl, Julia. Elizabeth knew Julia loved flowers. But Julia was sick and not able to tend her own little plot in her mom's garden. That afternoon, Elizabeth heard Julia telling her mom about the "lovely surprise" she'd found on her porch that morning. Elizabeth just smiled.

It's fun to surprise people with good things and not let them know who did it. We shouldn't do things to be admired by others. God wants us to do things for Him, not to make others like us or to receive praise from them. God will reward us when we give in secret.

⊙ Hold That Thought ⊙

Ask God to give you an idea for something special you can do secretly for someone. Take joy in giving secret surprises—and in the fact that God sees what you do.

DAY 9

The Full Reward

Be diligent so that you will receive your full reward.
2 John 1:8

For each weekday that Nick worked on his math during the summer, his parents paid him one dollar. Nick had the opportunity to earn sixty dollars that summer. But some days, Nick slacked off and chose not to do his homework. By the time school started, he had earned thirty-four dollars.

Now, thirty-four dollars is better than nothing; but Nick had the potential to earn much more. In the same way, we have the opportunity to gain many heavenly rewards. But in order to earn our full reward, we must work diligently and live in a way that earns God's rewards each day.

◎ Hold That Thought ◎

Keep this thought with you today: By loving and serving Jesus with my whole heart, I can be sure to receive my full reward in heaven.

DAY 10

Rewards from Father

Every good and perfect gift is from above,
coming down from the Father of the heavenly lights.

James 1:17, NIV

Caden was adopted when he was ten. Before that, he never really had a home or a family. He had been hurt and scared most of his life, so at first he was angry with his new family all the time. Then slowly, as his new family continued to love him unconditionally, his anger began to fade.

One day he found a present on his bed. He took it downstairs and asked, "What's this? It's not Christmas, and my birthday was months ago."

His dad said, "You're part of our family now, and we wanted to give you something special." Caden eagerly unwrapped the present. The gift was a Bible, and inside was a family tree with names written in. Right there was Caden's name, printed alongside the names of his new brother and sister.

"Wow." Caden was quiet for a moment. He ran his fingers over the leather cover, then looked up at his parents. "How can I ever thank you?"

"You're our son now," his mom said. "Just saying thank you is enough."

Like Caden, God has adopted everyone who believes in Jesus as His sons and daughters. God is the best Father you can imagine, and He gives us wonderful gifts—just because He loves us so much.

STAFF

◎ Hold That Thought ◎

What gifts has God given to you? A family? Friends? A pet? Your home? Make a list of everything you can think of. Then thank Him for His gifts of love to you.

⊙ Hold That Thought ⊙

Have you experienced some
hard times lately? Does it ever
feel like God is far away?
During those times, God
wants you to come to Him.
He will always be there for
you, in good times and bad.

Make Us Stronger

*If your faith remains strong after being
tried by fiery trials, it will bring you much praise
and glory and honor on the day when
Jesus Christ is revealed to the whole world.*

1 Peter 1:7

I know an older woman named Sally, who is one of the godliest people I have ever met. Every minute of her life is about Jesus. Every breath, every step she takes is because of Him. I told Sally once that sometimes I feel like God is far away. "How have you become so close to Him?" I asked.

Sally smiled, and then she sat there for a moment in thoughtful silence. "Many years of getting to know Him," she said. "But mostly it was through sad, hard times when Jesus was my only friend. During those trials is when He and I became really close."

The Bible says that hard things happen to make our faith stronger. You may have experienced the death of a family member. Perhaps a friend has moved away. Or maybe your parents have been divorced. As painful as these things are, they can bring you closer to Jesus. And when you stay close by His side through tough times, He will help you and make you strong. So instead of running away when times get tough, be like Sally and run to God.

Let's Celebrate!

Jesus told His workers:

"Let's celebrate together!"
Matthew 25:23

Travis had nothing planned that Saturday. The fourteen-year-old was sitting on his front lawn, trying to think of something exciting to do when his neighbor walked up the pathway. "Are you busy today?" John asked. "Because if you aren't, I could really use your help."

Travis shrugged his shoulders. "Sure. I have nothing to do anyway."

Travis followed John to his garage where they got out a lawn-mower, a hedge trimmer, and a hose. "If you can start by mowing the lawn, I'll work on the bushes. Then we can both water the flower beds."

At first, Travis was asking himself, *Why in the world am I using up my whole Saturday to help my neighbor?* But as the day wore on, Travis discovered that he was actually having fun. A couple of times they stopped for a break, and John's wife, Amy, brought them some cool lemonade and homemade cookies. Later, while watering the flower beds, John and Travis got into a water fight. By early afternoon, the whole backyard was in tip-top shape.

"Now let's get the lawn chairs out and set up some tables," John said.

Travis raised his eyebrows. "I'm having a family barbecue tonight," John explained. "And you've been such a big help to me today. How would you like to join us? Amy's been cooking like crazy, and I was thinking about setting up the volleyball net, too. What do you say?"

Travis was glad he had decided to help.

When we come to God with willing hearts and do what He asks, He will invite us to celebrate with Him for eternity in heaven. Jesus says He has prepared a place for those who love Him (1 Corinthians 2:9). So come celebrate with Jesus and see what He has in store for you!

☺ Hold That Thought ☺

What do you imagine heaven's celebration will be like? Do you picture a massive table full of food, a huge lawn for playing on, and maybe even rainbows to slide down? Thank God that you've already received your invitation because you have trusted in Jesus.

DAY 13

Expected Results

Jesus said:

*"Every tree that does not produce good fruit
will be cut down and thrown into the fire."*
Matthew 3:10, NIV

What is your favorite school subject? Math, or maybe reading? (Recess and lunch don't count as subjects!) In school you learn about history, and then you take a test to see what you remember. But what if you studied the same lesson the whole year? What if every test was the same every time? Yes, it would be easy, but after a while it would be kind of silly and boring. Thankfully, that's not how it works in school, and that's not how God wants us to live either. He wants us to get to know Him better—to grow and love Him and His people more and more. He doesn't want us to stay the same every day, never growing or doing anything for Him. He wants to see results, and He promises to reward us when we achieve results.

⊙ **Hold That Thought** ⊙

Are you growing in God today? Are you learning new things from Him? As you do your best for Him and grow closer to Him, you will see wonderful results in your life.

DAY 14

Tell His Story

Paul once wrote:

I pray that you may be active in sharing your faith.
Philemon 1:6, NIV

Imagine for a second that you're in heaven. Who is there with you? Whose faces do you see? What about the people you know whose faces you don't see there? You hope they are on their way…but hoping isn't enough.

None of us knows when it will be our time to go to heaven. Think about this: Every conversation you have with someone who doesn't know Christ might be the last conversation you ever have. Suddenly, telling others about Jesus seems a lot more important than ever before.

Yes, sometimes it is hard to tell people, even close friends, about Jesus. But the thought of their not being with you in heaven is very sad. As followers of Christ, we should share our faith with others every day. Don't you want to tell your friends about Jesus so that together you can spend forever in heaven?

☉ Hold That Thought ☉

Think of your friends and family members who don't know Jesus. Pray for them. Ask God to give you the opportunity and courage to tell them about Jesus and His great love for them.

DAY 15

Snowflakes and Hope

"For I know the plans I have for you," says the LORD. "They are plans for good and not for disaster, to give you a future and a hope."
Jeremiah 29:11

Think about how many snowflakes fall each winter. Yet each snowflake has its own shape and design, and God created them all. It's pretty awesome to realize how creative God is!

We are kind of like snowflakes. Each of us is special and unique and unlike any other person. We each have our own design—what we're good at, what makes us smile, what's hard for us, what makes us cry. And though there are billions of people here on earth, God knows and loves each and every one of us.

And even more amazing is the fact that He has devised a plan for each of our lives! Some of us will be firefighters, some teachers. Others will sing, and some will preach God's Word. Some of us will get married, and some of us will be missionaries in other lands. Whatever God has planned for you, you don't need to worry. He's thought about you since before you were born, and He has a plan full of hope for you!

☉ Hold That Thought ☉

What are your plans for the future? Learning a musical instrument? Playing a new sport? Running for a political office? God knows exactly what the future holds for you. Thank Him for His plan and ask Him to help you follow it.

DAY 16

Making a Difference

Jesus said:

*"I know all the things you do.
I have seen your hard work
and your patient endurance."*

Revelation 2:2

Jacob and Tara lived in southern Texas near the Mexican border. Many weekends they would go with their parents across the border to take food and clothing to those in need. Often, the food they brought would be the only food some of the Mexican children had eaten in a couple of days. Jacob and Tara were sad to see children almost starving. This made it hard to go there sometimes. And it was easy to get discouraged, because no matter how much food they brought or how many times they went, there were always many more families who needed help.

But Jacob and Tara's dad reminded them that they were making a difference. They were showing God's love to many families and children, and Jacob and Tara would one day see many of these same people in heaven—maybe because Jacob and Tara had first helped them to see Jesus.

☙ Hold That Thought ☙

Do you ever feel like you aren't making a difference with the things you do? Guess what? Jesus sees and He knows. And He will reward you for working hard and being patient. Ask God to help you to keep living for Him.

DAY 17

A Privilege and an Honor

You have been given not only the privilege of trusting in Christ but also the privilege of suffering for him.

Philippians 1:29

You have probably been given a special privilege before. Maybe you got to stay up past your bedtime for a family gathering or to watch a special program. Maybe you got to go golfing with your grandpa. Or maybe your mom said you could spend the night at a friend's house on a school night. Those are all privileges, special things you were allowed to do.

The Bible says we are privileged to suffer for Jesus. At first that may sound crazy. Who wants to suffer for somebody else? But it is a privilege. God only asks some of us to suffer for Him. A few have died in foreign lands for telling people about Jesus, while others have been beaten and put in prison smuggling Bibles into places where the Word of God is forbidden. The rewards for these people will be great in heaven.

So if God asks you to suffer for His Son, remember that it is a big honor: The God of the entire universe considers you worthy to suffer for Him! So instead of being afraid of suffering, welcome it, because it's for Jesus.

⊙ Hold That Thought ⊙

You may have always thought of privileges as being only fun things. But it is also a privilege to tell others about Christ, especially when you are insulted or even punished for doing it. Remember to pray for your church missionaries as they go into the world to tell people about Jesus.

DAY 18

Big Boy

Jesus said:

"You have remained loyal to me."
Revelation 2:13

Danni's family had owned Big Boy since before Danni was born. Big Boy was a beautiful black Labrador retriever, and he and Danni were best buds. Everywhere Danni went, Big Boy followed. And if he couldn't go inside, Big Boy waited patiently by the door for Danni. One time, Danni went to her cousin's house and left Big Boy at the back door, forgetting that she'd brought her dog along. Big Boy waited patiently for hours, until Danni finally remembered and returned for him.

Whatever Danni ate, Big Boy ate, too, whether it was broccoli or ice cream. If Danni threw a stick or a Frisbee, Big Boy would search until he found the stick or the Frisbee. Once he even climbed up a tree and broke his tail—but he got the Frisbee!

Big Boy was as loyal as a brother or a best friend to Danni. Jesus wants us to be that loyal to Him. And you know what? He shows the same kind of loyalty to us each and every day.

◎ Hold That Thought ◎

What comes to mind when you hear the word loyalty? You may think of your own dog or a special friend. Being loyal to Jesus means faithfully following Him wherever He leads. Today, pray that God will help you be loyal to Him.

DAY 19

Hold On!

God commands us:

Hold on to what is good.
1 Thessalonians 5:21

Julee and her best friends would soon be entering junior high, and they all wanted to stay friends. They regularly got together to pray for each other and to help people in their town. They knew that this was a good thing, and each of them wanted to keep it going in junior high. Despite hectic schedules and activities like volleyball, piano lessons, and gymnastics, the girls always made time to get together for prayer and community service projects. Julee and her friends chose to hold on to what was good.

When we get busy, it's easy to let what is good and important slip away, but God doesn't want that to happen. "Hold on to what is good," He said. There's a whole lot of bad stuff in this world, so you have to fight for the good. Are you ready and willing to hold on to what is good, even if you have to make sacrifices for it?

☉ Hold That Thought ☉

Think of three good things in your life that are worth holding on to. Your list may include a friend who is always there for you, your Sunday school class, or talks you have with your mom. Ask Jesus to help you hold on to the good things He has provided for you.

DAY 20

A Sure Winner

Now thanks be to God who always leads us in triumph in Christ.
2 Corinthians 2:14, NKJV

What if Traci knew she would win her tae kwon do match every time, even if she was fighting someone bigger and more experienced? What if a country knew it would win every war it fought, even if the enemy was bigger and better equipped? What if you knew you could beat any competitor in a race, even if she were an Olympic athlete?

If Traci knew she would win every match, don't you think she would have a lot of confidence in her skills? If a country's government knew it would win every war, wouldn't they be more forceful in voicing their opinions, knowing they could back them up? And how would it feel to know you would win every race, no matter who the opponent?

Even though it's likely that Traci won't win all her matches, a country won't win every war, and you will not be faster than everyone you race, there is one victory you can count on every time.

Jesus will always win, and in fact, He has already won. He is the victor, and He leads His people in triumph. Imagine what rewards and celebration there will be for everyone who's on His side!

☉ Hold That Thought ☉

What does victory mean to you? How does it feel to win a race or a game? Sometimes you don't win, right? But in Jesus we always have a winner. He proved Himself victorious over death, making those who believe in Him champions for all eternity! Thank Him for His triumph. Ask Him to lead you each and every day.

DAY 21

Rainbows

David wrote this:

Praise the LORD, I tell myself;
with my whole heart,
I will praise his holy name.

Psalm 103:1

Macy sat on the swing in her backyard, staring up at the huge rainbow she knew God had put there. All of a sudden Macy started singing "Jesus Loves Me" as loud as she could! She felt like God had put the rainbow there just for her. *I know that God doesn't want me to praise Him only when I am in church or feeling good,* she thought. Sometimes at school she didn't think about God at all. "But I want to change that," she said quietly to herself. "I want Jesus to be in all of my life, and I want to praise Him with my whole heart." Then she asked God to help her. God longs for us to love Him and give Him our whole life. He loves us so much, and He always welcomes our praise.

☺ Hold That Thought ☺

How often do you praise Jesus? Do you sing songs of praise only when you are at church, or do you praise Him at home, too? Today, tell Him from your heart that you love Him for who He is and for what He has done in your life.

God's Journal

David sang to God:

Every day of my life was recorded in your book.
Psalm 139:16

There was once an old sea captain who wrote down all of his experiences in a log, or journal. Every day he took notes on the weather, describing the behavior of the wind and the sea. He wrote about his crew and how they were getting along. The captain also expressed his thoughts, feelings, and emotions in his log. Some days he felt lonely, and he cried out to God with his pen and thanked Him for being his friend. On days when the sunshine outside matched the sunshine in his heart, he praised God for providing him with the ocean breeze and a beautiful ship to sail the seas.

Like the old sea captain, God keeps a journal. In this journal is recorded every thought, every action, and every feeling of every person that ever lived. Can you imagine how big His journal is? When Jesus comes back for us, God's journal will be opened for all to see. Jesus will read the journal His Father so carefully kept, and the Bible tells us that we will be held accountable for our every thought and action. Let's live in a way that we will not be ashamed of when God's journal is read out loud someday in heaven.

☺ Hold That Thought ☺

Psalm 94:11 says that "the LORD knows the thoughts of man" (NIV). What thoughts of yours has God been recording lately? Are they things you can be proud of, or do you need to ask God to help you change your thoughts into ones that honor Him? Ask God today to be the author of your thoughts and actions, so that when your story is read before all of heaven, you won't be ashamed.

The First and the Last

Jesus said:

"Do not be afraid. I am the First and the Last."
Revelation 1:17, NIV

Toby's family moved to a new city during Christmas vacation. In January, Toby would enroll in a new school in the middle of the school year. The only person she knew in the area was her older brother, Mike. On the morning of the first day, Toby was a little nervous as she was getting ready. To her surprise, her brother told her he would drive her to school.

"What about your classes?" Toby asked.

"I asked my first-period teacher if I could be late, and he said it was okay."

That day Mike helped Toby find her locker and her classroom. Mike told her he would be waiting for her after school. That thought comforted Toby throughout the day.

Jesus watches out for us like Toby's brother did. Jesus is the first and the last. He walks ahead of us and behind us, so we have nothing to fear. He is the beginning and the end, and He promises blessings for all those who walk with Him—too many blessings to count!

☺ Hold That Thought ☺

Think about this today: Jesus is always with me, from beginning to end, start to finish.

Age Doesn't Matter

John wrote:

I am writing to you who are young because you have won your battle with Satan.... I have written to you who are young because you are strong with God's word living in your hearts, and you have won your battle with Satan.

1 John 2:13–14

Who are the winners for God? Who are the champions who inherit the greatest rewards in heaven?

You can be one of them. Yes, you are young. But you are strong. God's Word is living in your heart. Let it grow there.

Kari believed the verse that said, "Don't let anyone look down on you because you are young" (1 Timothy 4:12, NIV). Ever since she was four and a missionary family came to her church, she knew that missions was what God wanted her to do. Sometimes people would try to tell Kari to wait until she was older to decide, but Kari never changed her mind. She knew God had spoken to her, even though she was so young at the time.

Just like Kari listened to God about one day becoming a missionary, God wants you to listen to Him, too. God is just waiting for you to say yes to Him. He's waiting for you to let Him use you. When you do, your reward will be great on earth and in heaven!

☉ Hold That Thought ☉

The Bible doesn't say you must wait until a certain age to really love Jesus and live for Him. God says that when you are young, you are strong. He wants to use you right now. Ask Him today to use you and make you strong in Him.

Made for Heaven

Praise for God:

*You will keep on guiding me with your counsel,
leading me to a glorious destiny.*

Psalm 73:24

There was once a very old, wise man. He lived in a little village surrounded by farmland. Everybody in the village went to the old man for advice, to ask questions, and to settle disputes.

Every day a young boy named Chris visited the wise man; Chris was eager to learn from him. Sometimes Chris would come with questions and the wise man would answer them. Sometimes Chris would just listen to the man talk about many different things.

The years passed and Chris grew up, but still he went every day to the wise man's house. And then one day the wise man told Chris that it was his time to die, but that it was okay because Chris himself had grown into a very wise man. A few days later the wise old man passed away. He left behind instructions for Chris to replace him as the counselor and wise man in the village.

If you ask, God will give you wisdom. He will show you what to do, where to go, and how to live your whole life until one day you arrive in the place He has prepared just for you. What a glorious day that will be, when we finally reach our true home, our glorious home with God in heaven!

> ☺ **Hold That Thought** ☺
>
> Ask God today to guide you in everything you do. Ask for His wisdom, and He will gladly give it to you.

God or Rewards?

All will be well for those who are godly. Tell them,
"You will receive a wonderful reward."
Isaiah 3:10

Damon was an excellent skier. Even when he was a little boy, his coaches and parents talked about his participating in the Winter Olympics someday. He was that good! As for Damon, instead of thinking about what he could win someday, he just focused on doing what he loved. He believed that if he kept on skiing just because he truly loved it, then all the awards and medals would naturally follow. And he was right.

Instead of working hard for rewards with our focus on what we can get, God wants us to think about Him. God wants us to love Him, not His rewards. If we will seek God first, all the other things will be given to us as well. But loving God is the most important thing you can do in this life.

The Bible says God rewards those who love Him and look to Him in all they do. So go hard after the Lord—seek Him, pursue Him, follow Him—and you won't be missing out on any of His rewards.

⊚ Hold That Thought ⊚

Remember: If we ever get to taking pleasure in the treasure and not the Treasurer, there's no treasure at all.

Spelling out the Future

Don't envy sinners, but always continue to fear the LORD. For surely you have a future ahead of you; your hope will not be disappointed.
Proverbs 23:17–18

Sometimes it's tempting for Jenna to want to cheat in school. Spelling is her hardest subject; no matter how much she studies, she never seems to get the words right. A couple of other girls in Jenna's class cheat on the tests and get away with it. At times, it's tempting to join them, but Jenna knows that would be wrong. So she chooses to keep on studying, even though she may never get grades as good as the girls who cheat.

But guess who will win in the end? Jenna will, and not just because she was honest. Because she didn't cheat, she actually had to learn how to spell. In the end, the cheaters were not only dishonest but also remained poor spellers. Looking back, Jenna was glad she did the right thing.

Sometimes it seems like those who do wrong are gaining more than those who do right. But the Bible tells us to continue following God's path. You have a hope and a future in Him that won't disappoint you.

☉ Hold That Thought ☉

Imagine this ad in the classified section of your newspaper:

THE BEST FUTURE EVER: Custom designed just for you by your Creator and purchased for you by His Son, Jesus Christ. Follow the Holy Spirit for day-to-day instructions. GUARANTEED FOR ALL ETERNITY.

Will you answer this ad today?

Now and Forever

Everything belongs to you... the whole world and life and death;
the present and the future. Everything belongs to you,
and you belong to Christ, and Christ belongs to God.

1 Corinthians 3:21–23

Most of what the Bible says about rewards has to do with heaven. Most of our rewards from God are something we must wait for until we arrive there. But God also lets us enjoy rewards even now.

One day, when the disciples were with Jesus, they were thinking and talking about all they had given up to follow Him. They were wondering what rewards they would receive from God.

Jesus answered them, "I assure you that everyone who has given up house or brothers or sisters or mother or father or children or property, for my sake and for the Good News, will receive now in return, a hundred times over.... And in the world to come they will have eternal life" (Mark 10:29–30).

Did you see that word *now?* Even now, we can enjoy amazing rewards from God. This is true for every believer. We can enjoy amazing peace with God. We are surrounded by other Christians who love and encourage us. And we are given the Holy Spirit to work in our hearts and our lives.

And this is just the beginning!

⊙ Hold That Thought ⊙

What are some of the other rewards that God has given you to enjoy here and now? Thank Him for each one and praise Him for His faithfulness!

DAY 29

To Live or Die?

Paul said this:

For to me, living is for Christ, and dying is even better.
Philippians 1:21

One day Carlie and Dave were talking about dying. "I don't know if I would die for someone," Carlie said.

"I would," Dave said, "especially for Jesus, since He died for me. I think it would be kind of cool to die for Him."

Carlie raised her eyebrows. "Cool to die?"

"Well, if you live your life completely for Jesus," said Dave, "and someone threatens to kill you because of your faith, why stop loving Jesus then? Isn't it better to die than to go on living, knowing you had forsaken Jesus?"

"I guess so," Carlie said. "I'm just glad we live where we don't have to choose between living and loving Jesus."

"There are places around the world where people are killed for believing in Jesus, Carlie. And who knows? Someday things might change here, too. Do you think you'd be ready?"

"Only if God helped me," Carlie said.

⊙ Hold That Thought ⊙

What about you? Would you be willing to die for Jesus? Just remember, God will always give you the help and strength you need for everything you will ever face—in life and in death.

DAY 30

The Boogeyman?
God Is Much Bigger!

The word of the LORD came to Abram in a vision.
"Do not be afraid, Abram. I am your shield, your very great reward."
Genesis 15:1, NIV

Every night when she was little, Aubrey would start running at her bedroom door and leap to her bed from as far away as possible. She was afraid that a boogeyman lived under her bed and that if she got too close, he would grab her foot and pull her under. Sounds kind of silly, maybe, but don't we all have secret fears like Aubrey's? Some people hate being alone in the dark; others have a fear of heights.

But God tells us not to be afraid of anything because He is our protection. No boogeyman stands a chance. What an encouraging thought! Aubrey doesn't have to jump into bed now (unless she wants to for the fun of it), and you can brave dark hallways at night. Have no fear! God is your shield and reward.

⊙ Hold That Thought ⊙

Perfect love casts out fear, the Bible says. Today, allow God's love to grow in you. Ask Him to lead you to greater strength and confidence in Him.

May 2003

S	M	T	W	T	F	S
				1	2	3
4	5	6	7	8	9	10
11	12	13	14	15	16	17
18	19	20	21	22	23	24
25	26	27	28	29	30	31

June 2003

S	M	T	W	T	F	S
1	2	3	4	5	6	7
8	9	10	11	12	13	14
15	16					28
22	23					
29	30					

July 2003

S	M	T	W	T	F	S
		1	2	3		
6	7	8	9	10	11	12
13	14	15	16	17	18	19
20	21	22	23	24	25	26
27	28	29	30	31		

August 2003

S	M	T	W	T	F	S
					1	2
3	4	5	6	7	8	9
10	11	12	13	14	15	16
17	18	19	20	21	22	23
24	25	26	27	28	29	30
31						

PART THREE

PART III

What God Is Looking For

What kind of "good things" will God reward? How can you know when you are pleasing God? How can you know when you are doing the kinds of things He wants you to do?

What about the things you do that God calls worthless? What about when you're bored? How can you keep from doing things that will not earn any rewards from God?

Let God show you His answers to these questions. Find out how even the little things you do each day will make a difference forever.

DAY 1

Today's the Day

The Lord promises:

"I will guide you along the best pathway for your life."
Psalm 32:8

Thousands of years ago, before the earth was created—before there were cities, cars, and people—God was in heaven. And He thought about you and your life. He created an exciting plan for you and for every day of your life. You may feel uncertain of your future, like an explorer heading off to chart the Antarctic or an Amazon jungle or a region of space that no one has ever seen before—but God has seen it all, and He knows just where you're going. If you stick with Him and follow His ways, you'll find that living by God's plan is a wonderful adventure!

Your adventure starts today. God wants you to walk the path He's mapped out for you. When you follow His path, it leads to even more rewarding adventures—not only in your life on earth, but with God in heaven! Keep talking to Him in prayer and reading His Word to discover what He has in store for you.

☼ Hold That Thought ☼

You want the real thing, don't you? Real adventure? God wants that for you, too. Can you trust Him for that? Let Him know. Talk to Him about the adventure He has planned for you.

His Arms Are Full!

Yes, the Sovereign LORD is coming in all his glorious power.
He will rule with awesome strength.
See, he brings his reward with him as he comes.

Isaiah 40:10

Pretend your parents are vacationing on a tropical island. They've been gone for two weeks and will be back today. You get to meet them at the airport. You can't wait! They have promised to bring you a present, too. They'll soon be walking off the plane, their arms full of gifts for family and friends. Can you guess what your present will be? A T-shirt with a volcano on it? A purse filled with exotic candy? A giant poster of the island?

Like your parents, Jesus is coming back soon, too. But this isn't pretend. When He comes, He too will have His arms full of gifts. And the more you've been able to do for Him, the greater the rewards He will be able to give you. Get ready. He's coming!

☼ Hold That Thought ☼

Jesus is coming. Jesus will soon be here with rewards for us. Take a moment today to look up into the sky and picture His coming. Imagine seeing Him there. Tell Jesus how excited you are for Him to come.

DAY 3

Who's on Your Guest List?

Jesus said:

*"At the resurrection of the godly,
God will reward you for inviting those
who could not repay you."*

Luke 14:14

Have you ever invited one of your friends over for dinner?
Did she later invite you over to her house? Not everyone you
know can return your meal invitation. Guess what Jesus says
about that? He wants us to invite into our homes the poor,
crippled, the lame, and the blind—people who can't pay us
back. When we do this, we will be rewarded in heaven.
Maybe the next time you have a sleepover, you can invite the
girl at school who nobody talks to. Or when you have
friends over to play volleyball, you can invite the girl who
always gets chosen last for teams at school. When we reach
out to others, God will reward us.

☼ Hold That Thought ☼

Plan to host a dinner with
your mom. Think about who
should be on your guest list.
Ask God to show you other
ways you can brighten the day
of someone who cannot pay
you back.

DAY 4

The Place of Power

Jesus said:

"And in the future you will see me, the Son of Man, sitting at God's right hand in the place of power and coming back on the clouds of heaven."

Matthew 26:64

Mandi and Josh tiptoed away from the church sanctuary, trying not to giggle too loudly. They had decided to play a joke. It was Sunday morning, and the services hadn't started yet. Mandi and Josh had taken all the Bibles and replaced them with Bibles that were written in Spanish. Now all they had to do was sneak away. But when they went around a corner, they bumped into the one person they didn't want to see—Pastor Greg. Immediately, they both stopped laughing because they knew that Pastor Greg had the power and authority to get them in deep trouble. Mandi and Josh apologized to Pastor Greg. He didn't get upset. He simply told them that they needed to put the Bibles back where they belonged before church started. He even helped them do it!

Someday soon we will be in heaven, and it is Jesus who will be our judge. He is the one with the power, and our future in heaven will be in His hands.

☼ Hold That Thought ☼

Remember this today: I will show respect to my parents and to all the people that God has placed in power and authority in my life.

Dust and Forever

God said to man:

"For dust you are, and to dust you shall return."
Genesis 3:19, NKJV

Remember the story of Adam and Eve? God specifically told them not to eat from a certain tree in the Garden of Eden, but they did just that. Have you ever disobeyed the instruction of your parents or God? All of us have, and we have learned that there are consequences when we disobey.

One of the consequences of Adam and Eve's disobedience was that their bodies would become dust when they died. We will all die someday. But even though we die and our bodies turn to dust, the "real us" will live on. And when we are part of God's family, there is a wonderful eternity ahead of us—an eternity longer than ten lives or even ten thousand. Isn't it great to know that even though your earthly body will disappear, you will still live forever? If you live your life loving God on this earth, it will affect you every day in heaven. You'll be so glad you did—forever and always!

☼ Hold That Thought ☼

Death can be a scary thought, but remember that death is only a doorway to an eternity with Jesus. Thank God that you will get to be with Him in heaven forever.

DAY 6

Standing Alone

David sang these words to God:

Surely you judge all people according to what they have done.

Psalm 62:12

Brittany and Janice were best friends. They liked to hang out together, but they sometimes got into trouble. One day they dressed up in costumes and told a little neighbor girl that they were kidnappers who were going to steal her away forever; the little girl ran away screaming and crying. As the little girl's screams echoed through the neighborhood, Brittany and Janice ran to Brittany's room and hid themselves. Brittany's mother knew right away that something was up, and the story soon came out. She sent Janice home, but she sent Brittany alone to confess and apologize to the little girl and her mother.

That's how it will be when we get to heaven. Each of us will stand alone—not with our best friend, our mom, or our dog. We will have to tell God why we did the things we did. If you think it was hard for Brittany, imagine how hard it will be to tell God about lying to your teacher or being mean to your brother. It makes you think twice about what you do!

☼ Hold That Thought ☼

Have you ever had to confess something you did wrong? It's not easy, is it? Let's do things that please God today, so that one day when we meet Him in person, He will say to us, "Well done!"

DAY 7

Tell the World

Jesus said:

"Go into all the world and preach the Good News to everyone, everywhere."

Mark 16:15

Have you heard of people going on missions trips around the world? Usually they travel to a poor country and tell people about Jesus while bringing them food, clothes, and medicine. Jesus told us to go into all the world to tell people how much God loves them. Some think they have to go to a foreign country to do this, but that's not so. Wherever you are is the perfect place to tell people about Jesus!

When you share the good news about Jesus—in another country or with your friends—you can also let them know about the rewards that He gives to those who follow Him. Don't keep the good news about rewards in heaven to yourself. Let everybody know!

☼ Hold That Thought ☼

Do you have a friend or relative who doesn't know Jesus? Ask God to prepare the way for you to share Jesus' message with him or her. Ask Him to work in that person's heart so that you can tell the good news about what Jesus has done in your life.

DAY 8

Now or Later?

Then at last everyone will say, "There truly is a reward for those who live for God; surely there is a God who judges justly here on earth."

Psalm 58:11

I don't know many people who like getting shots, but six-year-old Bryan is one kid who absolutely hates them! One day, Bryan's mom took him to the doctor's office to get a shot, but when he saw the needle he threw a tantrum. No matter what they said, Bryan continued to scream, hit, and kick every time the nurse came near him with the needle. At last, Bryan's mom got tired of trying to convince him to hold still and got a few adults to help hold him down. As much as Bryan tried to fight it, this time he couldn't move; the nurse finally gave him the shot. Despite all his struggling, fighting, and begging, Bryan still ended up getting the shot. If he had let the nurse give him the shot right away, he would have avoided a lot of trouble!

Like Bryan, we each face a choice in our lives. We can either fight God now and one day submit to Him, or we can live for Him now and then be rewarded for it in heaven. So what do you say? The choice is yours.

☼ Hold That Thought ☼

Are you ever stubborn or resistant? Instead of following someone else's directions, would you rather just do things your own way? It isn't always easy to follow the Word of God. But when you do, you'll find that it makes a lot of sense for today—and will lead to rewards beyond what you can imagine in heaven!

DAY 9

Christmas in Heaven

Jesus said:

*"Rejoice in that day and leap for joy,
because great is your reward in heaven."*

Luke 6:23, NIV

It's Christmas morning. The sun has barely risen. All the beautifully wrapped presents are under the tree, and each stocking is filled to the top with goodies and toys. You open your eyes, look at the clock, and wonder why you woke up so early. Then you remember. It's Christmas! You jump out of bed and start yelling, "Wake up, everybody! It's Christmas! Wake up!" Does that sound familiar? Suddenly, the whole house is full of excited voices and echoing footsteps as everyone hurries toward the tree.

God wants us to feel just as excited about our rewards in heaven. And why shouldn't we? We can't even begin to imagine what heaven will be like, but we know that it will be better than anything we've ever dreamed of! The moment we enter eternity will truly be a time to "leap for joy"!

☼ Hold That Thought ☼

What do you get most excited about? Playing soccer? Getting into a good book? Having friends over for your birthday party? Although we can't understand it now, being in heaven and seeing the rewards that God has been preparing for you will be more exciting than anything you've done or seen before.

God Will Not Forget

God is not unfair. He will not forget how hard
you have worked for him and how you have shown your love
to him by caring for other Christians.

Hebrews 6:10

Bradley and Cassie were each given a job to do while their mom and dad went to town. Bradley's task was to paint a fence with his older brother, and Cassie was supposed to weed the garden. Their parents promised to bring them back a surprise if they finished their chores.

Bradley and Cassie worked hard to complete their assignments. When their parents returned, the fence was painted and the garden weeded.

"Where's our surprise?" the kids asked.

"Oh no! We forgot, but we'll get you something soon," their father said. A few days passed, and then a few more. Soon, Bradley and Cassie gave up on getting a surprise.

Has someone ever forgotten how hard you worked? It isn't fair, is it? But you know what? God isn't like that. He never forgets His promises. He always remembers and rewards His children for the good things they've done. You can count on it.

☼ Hold That Thought ☼

Thank God for seeing and remembering every good thing you do for Him—even if no one else notices.

DAY 11

Meeting with the Principal

Jesus said:

*"And the Father leaves all judgment to his Son,
so that everyone will honor the Son,
just as they honor the Father."*

John 5:22–23

Michelle and Jonathan were both told to visit the principal's office after school. Neither had any idea why, but they wondered if they had gotten into trouble somehow. When the principal walked by Michelle and Jonathan that day in the cafeteria, they both sat up a little straighter. They knew that they would be talking to him later, so they were extra careful to be on their best behavior. When the school day ended and Michelle and Jonathan finally met with the principal, they found they weren't in trouble at all! The principal just wanted to tell them what a good job they had done in the school play the week before.

One day, Jesus will be our judge. God planned it that way so that people would honor His Son. Like Michelle and Jonathan meeting the principal, we need to remember that one day we are going to meet with Jesus. When that happens, will He be telling us "Good job!"?

☼ Hold That Thought ☼

Jesus said the reason He had been given all authority to judge was so that everyone would honor Him. What kind of choices can you make that will honor Jesus?

DAY 12

He Died So You Can Live

*Jesus said, "It is finished." With that,
he bowed his head and gave up his spirit.*

John 19:30, NIV

When people say that Jesus died for you, it's easy to forget what that really means. He didn't just fall asleep and not wake up the next morning. He was killed in a most horrible and painful way. He had massive nails pounded into His hands and feet to hold Him on a cross. He hung there for hours and then finally said, "It is finished."

Then He died. And you know what? He died so that you and I could someday live in heaven with Him.

That fact should change how we live today and every day. He died so that you could truly live. So go live like He wants you to!

☼ Hold That Thought ☼

What does Jesus' death mean to you? Is it simply an event that you know about, or is it the way by which you can have a relationship with God? Talk to Jesus about His death and what He did for you.

For Good or for Evil

For we must all stand before Christ to be judged.
We will each receive whatever we deserve
for the good or evil we have done in our bodies.

2 Corinthians 5:10

Imagine if someone followed you around with a video camera your whole life and you could never escape it, no matter where you went or what you did. This video camera would be special—it would not only record everything you do, but it would also capture everything you think. All your mean or angry thoughts would suddenly be available for everyone to hear. Every word you muttered under your breath would be as loud as normal conversation.

Kind of scary to think about, isn't it? Of course, God doesn't follow us around with a camera and recorder, but He is God. He knows everything about us. One day, we will be judged for everything we have done in our lives. So watch what you do and remember that God sees everything.

☼ Hold That Thought ☼

Imagine that someone recorded your every thought and deed yesterday. What would your video reveal? Would you be proud of this one-day "episode" in your life? Would God be proud of it?

☼ Hold That Thought ☼

In Jesus, you and I have the
best fire insurance policy
there is! We can avoid loss in
heaven simply by choosing to
live for God and doing what
pleases Him today.

DAY 14

One Hot Fire!

The Bible warns us:

If the work is burned up, the builder will suffer great loss.
1 Corinthians 3:15

Leila walked through what used to be her house. Most of it was ashes now, but you could still see where everything had been. She walked through her room and closed her eyes. Her bed was gone, her dresser of clothes, her posters—everything. It had all burned up.

Leila stepped to where her bookshelf had stood. Something on the ground caught her eye, and she stooped down to investigate. She brushed away the ashes and let out a gasp. There before her was the little metal swan that her grandmother had given Leila on her tenth birthday. It was her only possession that had survived the fire.

In heaven there will be a fire, too. But it won't be out of control like the one that destroyed Leila's house. Some things will burn up just like Leila's bed and dresser. Other things, like Leila's swan, won't burn at all. What will be put into this fire is everything we've done in our life. The good things, like the swan, will last. But the worthless things will quickly turn to ashes.

The Bible says that if our work is burned, we will suffer loss. I sure don't want to miss out on rewards in heaven, do you? Let's make sure that what we're doing will survive that heavenly blaze. Let's live lives that will come through the fire all in one piece.

DAY 15

Something to Look Forward To

We are heirs—heirs of God and co-heirs with Christ.
Romans 8:17, NIV

Evelyn and Elaine were twins. They had both loved dolls since they were little girls. They still collected them and read magazines about dolls from around the world. Evelyn and Elaine's grandmother was as fond of dolls as they were. She had an amazing (and valuable) doll collection. And ever since they were young, Evelyn and Elaine had been told they would inherit Grandma's doll collection on their thirteenth birthday. Even though they still had many months left, they talked about the collection all the time. It was so much fun to look forward to!

Like Evelyn and Elaine, we have much to look forward to as children of God. He promises us a grand inheritance when we join Him in heaven. With God as our Father, just imagine how great our inheritance will be!

☼ Hold That Thought ☼

Is there anything special you're looking forward to? A family camping trip? Spending the night at a friend's house? A new CD by your favorite recording artist? Well, God has even greater things in store for you! Thank Him today for the inheritance He has waiting for you in heaven.

☀ Hold That Thought ☀

Sometimes it's hard to believe how much God loves us even when we sometimes misbehave. Think about the people you love most and how you are willing to forgive them even when they say or do something that makes you angry. God loves you even more than that. Pretty amazing, isn't it? Thank God right now for loving us more than we'll ever deserve.

DAY 16

Undeserved

The LORD will delight in being good to you.
Deuteronomy 30:9

Jeff and Andrea's dad brought home a surprise for each of them. Jeff got a new baseball and Andrea a new CD. The kids thanked their dad and gave him a big hug, but they seemed to be a little nervous about something.

"What's wrong, kids? Don't you like the presents?" their dad asked.

"No, Dad, the presents are awesome," Jeff said, looking down.

"I think we're feeling a little bad because…well, we've been fighting a lot today and haven't really been obeying Mom," Andrea said quietly. "I guess maybe we feel like we don't deserve these gifts."

"I see," their dad said. "Well, let me tell you something. I got these for you because I love you and wanted to give you something. It has nothing to do with whether you were good or bad today. You can keep the presents. Now let's go talk to Mom about what happened today, okay?"

That's how God operates, too. He loves being good to us and giving us gifts, even when we don't deserve them. God is awesome!

DAY 17

The Book of Your Life

Notice this:

And the books were opened.
Revelation 20:12, NIV

Let's say you were going to write a biography, a book about someone's life. You would probably go talk to that person's family, friends, and teachers. You would read anything that anyone had ever written about the person. And if this person was still alive, you would try to spend time with her. The more you learned about this person, the more accurate the book you'd be able to write.

The last book in the Old Testament, Malachi, tells us about a document that was being written in the presence of God. "In his presence, a scroll of remembrance was written to record the names of those who feared him and loved to think about him" (3:16). God has a book that contains records of everything a person does. In heaven, this book will be opened, and there will be no mistakes in it. No one will be able to argue about what is recorded there because everything written will be true. On that day when the book is opened, how will your story read? It's up to you.

☀ Hold That Thought ☀

Remember that the story of what you do today—and every day of your life—will one day be read aloud in heaven.

DAY 18

We Need Him!

Jesus made this promise:

*"God blesses those who realize their need for him,
for the Kingdom of Heaven is given to them."*

Matthew 5:3

Becky stood on her tiptoes and stretched her hand up as high as it would go. She was still a few feet short of the box she was trying to get off the top shelf. She pulled up a chair and stood on it, but she still couldn't get close enough. Then Becky thought of her family's thick phone book. She put it on the chair and climbed on top. Even then her fingers barely brushed the bottom of the box. Exasperated, she called loudly for her mom. Right away, her mom came and effortlessly pulled the box down from the high shelf. "Next time, just ask me and I'll get it for you," Becky's mom said.

Sometimes, like Becky, we stubbornly try to figure things out on our own. God wants us to admit that we can't do everything by ourselves and realize that we need His help. Without Jesus, we are in trouble. It's only because of Him that we are even living. Jesus says that the kingdom of heaven is given to those who realize their need for a Savior.

☼ Hold That Thought ☼

When you need something, what do you do? Do you try to do it all on your own, or do you ask for help from someone? God wants to help, and He is always available in your time of need. Ask Him to help you in everything you do today.

Extra Strength

Jesus made this promise:

"God blesses those who mourn, for they will be comforted."
Matthew 5:4

Have you ever cried yourself to sleep at night? Has someone you loved ever died or left you? Have you ever felt really lonely? Have you ever been sad for a long time and not really known why?

Sometimes life can be sad and unfair because there is so much sin and pain in our world. Yet when you are sad, Jesus promises that you will be comforted and blessed because of your sadness. God will give you the strength to "patiently endure" (2 Corinthians 1:6). That's good to know!

There is another purpose for our sadness. The more we are sad and discover God's comfort, the easier it is for us to show that comfort to others: "When others are troubled, we will be able to give them the same comfort God has given us" (2 Corinthians 1:4).

As hard as it is sometimes, remember that even sadness is part of God's wonderful plan for us—and that He is always there, waiting for us to run to Him.

☼ Hold That Thought ☼

Do you know someone who needs God's comfort today? Ask God how you can share His love with this person.

Two Kinds of Players

Jesus promises:

"God blesses those who are gentle and lowly,
for the whole earth will belong to them."

Matthew 5:5

Sisters Jessie and Jeri both played basketball almost from the day they could stand up. Before they were old enough to be on a team, they played in their driveway with friends. When they could finally play on a real team, both girls were very excited. But there was one big difference between them. Jessie was a very unselfish player. She nearly always passed the ball to her teammates, and if she made a good shot or play, she would just smile quietly and thank those that congratulated her. Jeri, however, loved being the center of attention. She rarely passed the ball, preferring to take most of the shots herself. Whenever someone said, "Good job!" she replied with a cocky, "Yeah, I know."

God doesn't like it when we are prideful like Jeri and act like we have everything figured out. God loves it when we are humble like Jessie and look to Him for our strength: "He shows favor to the humble" (James 4:6). To those who do this, God promises the whole earth!

☼ Hold That Thought ☼

Who do you feel more like, Jessie or Jeri? Do you keep a humble heart, or does pride sometimes creep in when people praise you for your accomplishments? Ask God to keep you humble. Thank Him for the blessings that come with humility.

☼ Hold That Thought ☼

Do you ever complain that life isn't fair? What Jesus experienced on the cross wasn't fair, either. In fact, if there were a "Life's Not Fair" contest, He would win easily. Jesus did nothing wrong during His life, but He was killed for everything we do wrong. Now that's a thought worth remembering.

Life Isn't Fair

Jesus made this promise:

*"God blesses those who are hungry
and thirsty for justice,
for they will receive it in full."*

Matthew 5:6

Don't you hate it when other kids cut in line and get away with it? Or when your older brother gets to see a movie that you don't? When that happens, we usually complain, "That's not fair!" And it may even be true. There is a lot of wrongdoing, injustice, and unfairness in this world.

There is something inside us that longs for truth and justice. We want things to be made right. Jesus promises that whoever longs for justice will someday truly see it. What an amazing day that will be! So next time you hear the words "not fair," remember that life on this earth might not be fair...but in heaven everything will be made right.

DAY 22

Mercy Again

Jesus promises:

"God blesses those who are merciful, for they will be shown mercy."
Matthew 5:7

The Jackson family was driving to the lake to go camping. Anna and her two brothers were in the backseat, crowded together. Her little brother, Elliott, had just gotten a new CD for his birthday, so he asked Anna if he could borrow her headphones and CD player.

"Sure," Anna said, "but please be careful with the headphones. You broke them last time." Elliott started listening to the CD, and Anna fell asleep. She woke up to the sounds of an argument.

"She told you to be careful!"

"I didn't mean to."

Quietly, Anna asked Elliott what had happened and how the headphones broke. "I'm sorry, Anna," he said. "I took them off for a while and forgot about them, and somehow they got smashed." Elliott looked ready to cry, and even though Anna was frustrated that her brother had broken the headphones again, she forgave him.

"I'm really sorry, Anna," Elliott said again.

"I know you are," she said, giving him a hug.

Despite what had happened, Anna showed her brother mercy. Instead of getting angry or yelling at him, she forgave him and was kind. When we are merciful to others, God says that we will be shown mercy in return.

☀ Hold That Thought ☀

Do you know the definition of mercy? It means that you have the power to punish the person who wronged you, but instead you have compassion on that person and do not demand justice. Ask God to give you a merciful heart today.

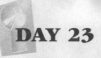

DAY 23

Pure and Clean

Jesus made this promise:

"God blesses those whose hearts are pure, for they will see God."
Matthew 5:8

As he lay in bed, Justin closed his eyes and frowned. He knew he needed to tell his dad that he'd broken the lawnmower. He'd been goofing around that morning, not watching where he was mowing, when he ran over a large rock that snapped off the blade. Afraid of what his dad would say, Justin had told him that the lawnmower was already broken when he'd taken it out of the garage. And now he felt guilty for lying.

Finally, Justin took a deep breath and went to look for his dad. He apologized and explained what had happened. His dad said that Justin would have to pay for the new blade—but he also gave him a hug and praised him for telling the truth. Later that night, Justin thought about how much better he felt after confessing to his dad.

Only when we confess our sins are we set free and made clean from them. Our sins stain our lives, and only Jesus can make us pure. So even when it's hard to admit your sins and ask for forgiveness, think about Jesus' promise: If your heart is pure, you will see God.

☼ Hold That Thought ☼

What have you done that you need God's forgiveness for? Have you hurt or wronged another person? Then you also need to ask that person to forgive you.

DAY 24

Children of God

Jesus promises:

*"God blesses those who work for peace,
for they will be called the children of God."*

Matthew 5:9

Peter, age four, was fascinated with models. He loved playing with all the little pieces and seeing how they might fit together. His older brother, Erik, had a large collection of model cars, ships, and planes. Peter would often sneak into Erik's room to look at them. One day Erik caught Peter playing with one of his favorite models, a jet plane he had recently finished. Erik yelled at Peter to put it back; Peter refused. Soon they were yelling and wrestling over the plane.

Their sister, Sonja, heard the commotion and hurried in. "Guys!" she yelled. "Stop!" Sonja rarely shouted, so the boys stopped. Sonja spoke more softly this time: "You guys are so loud I can't even read my book. Do you think God wants you to fight like this?" The boys didn't answer, but Peter slowly handed the plane back to his brother. Erik sighed. "Thank you, Peter," he said. Sonja smiled and walked away.

There is an amazing reward for everyone who helps people come together for God's sake. Jesus says they will be called God's children. Let's be peacemakers and show that we are part of God's family.

☼ Hold That Thought ☼

Do you know two people who are angry with one another about something? What can you do to help make peace between them today? Ask God for His help in this situation.

The Blessing in Being Hated

Jesus made this promise:

*"God blesses those who are persecuted
because they live for God,
for the Kingdom of Heaven is theirs."*
Matthew 5:10

Chloe knew that her classmates were upset with her. Actually, they were more than upset; Chloe was convinced that they hated her now. Some friends in her class had found a copy of the upcoming math test, and they were planning to use it to cheat. Chloe knew that wasn't what God wanted them to do, so she said she would not cheat. Chloe told them that God says cheating is wrong. The girls got really mad and refused to speak to her after that.

When Chloe made the decision to live for God and obey Him, she knew it would be hard. Being hated and persecuted is always hard, but God promises that He will reward us when that happens. He says that the kingdom of heaven belongs to Chloe and to others who are persecuted for Jesus. What about you? Are you willing to be mistreated and even hated for Jesus? Remember, He will bless you for it.

☀ Hold That Thought ☀

Have you ever been ignored or made fun of because of your faith in Jesus? It hurts, doesn't it? Tell Jesus about the pain, but at the same time thank Him for the privilege of being called a Christian.

☼ Hold That Thought ☼

Ask God to give you strength to endure the hardships you may face in His name. No matter what you're going through, He will never leave your side.

DAY 26

Glad for Suffering

Jesus promises:

*"God blesses you when you are mocked and persecuted
and lied about because you are my followers.
Be happy about it! Be very glad!
For a great reward awaits you in heaven."*
Matthew 5:11–12

In the Bible are many stories of people who were killed because they followed Jesus. Sometimes you and I are laughed at, teased, or maybe ignored because we follow Jesus—but killed? Why were these men of the Bible willing to die for Jesus?

Remember, most of the martyrs weren't killed quickly. Many were tortured, mocked, and murdered slowly in some of the worst ways imaginable. Yet in spite of this, the apostle Paul wrote, "For me, to live is Christ and to die is gain" (Philippians 1:21, NIV). He must have truly believed this with everything inside of him.

The martyrs in the Bible had an incredible promise straight from Jesus. A great reward awaited them in heaven because they followed Jesus, knowing that it could mean they would die a terrible death. And you know what? We have the same promise. There is a great reward in heaven for us when we suffer for Jesus. Jesus even tells us to "be very glad" about the chance to suffer for Him because of the great reward that awaits us. Our troubles today will melt away tomorrow. What an amazing God we serve!

God's Kingdom

Jesus told us to pray this to God our Father:

"May your kingdom come soon."
Matthew 6:10

Teresa could barely keep her eyes open. She tried to swallow her yawn, but it came out anyway. She had been up late the night before, and now she was having trouble staying awake in class. *I wonder what it would be like not to get tired,* Teresa thought. *It sure would be nice to be able to stay up late and then still be wide awake the next day.*

Maybe in heaven we won't get tired so easily; maybe we won't get tired at all! The Bible says that no one can even begin to think of what God has prepared for those who love Him. Jesus described it like this: "The Kingdom of Heaven is like a treasure that a man discovered hidden in a field. In his excitement, he hid it again and sold everything he owned to get enough money to buy the field—and to get the treasure, too!" (Matthew 13:44).

I can only imagine what heaven will be like. And I know that I want to be ready when the time comes for me to go there. Heaven sounds like a truly wonderful place, and I can't wait to see what it's like!

✺ Hold That Thought ✺

How do you picture heaven? Do you imagine grand mansions, shining lights, and golden streets? Whatever heaven is like, we know that being there with Jesus is a reward in itself.

DAY 28

Look to God

God… will supply all your needs from his glorious riches, which have been given to us in Christ Jesus.

Philippians 4:19

Lissa is a very special girl. The way she trusts in Jesus is amazing. Lissa's brain doesn't work the same way most people's do. It's hard for her to do math, even addition and subtraction, and she still can't read, even though she is ten. Yet Lissa understands a lot more about God than many people who are much older. Whenever she needs something, Lissa doesn't worry or get scared that it might not work out. She just tells God about it and asks Him to help. And the wonderful thing is that He always does. He is a loving Father who takes good care of His children, and Lissa knows she is His child.

God promises to supply all our needs. That doesn't mean that we send Him a wish list and He gives us everything we ever wanted. But He knows what we need and makes sure that we have it—both in our lives on earth and in heaven. Are you going to believe He will keep His promises, like Lissa does? He wants you to; He can't wait to give you everything you need.

☼ Hold That Thought ☼

Think of some of the things you want—maybe a bike, a horse, or a new tennis racket. Now think of some of the things you need. Maybe you have trouble understanding math and you need a tutor. Maybe you've been sick and you need God to make you well. Talk with God about the things you need and thank Him in advance for providing for you.

DAY 29

In His Hands

A promise from God:

There is surely a future hope for you,
and your hope will not be cut off.

Proverbs 23:18, NIV

Think about beautiful sunsets. Think about fishing on a lake so clear you can see all the way to the bottom. Think about the brilliant moon and millions of twinkling stars that fill the night sky. Think about the huge, crashing waves of the ocean. Think of the little caterpillar that turns into a colorful butterfly. Think about all these things. God created each one.

God is the Master of the universe, the world, and you. He has everything under control, from the farthest galaxies to the tiny ladybug just outside your bedroom window. You don't have to worry because your life, your hope, and your future are in His hands. God has a plan for each of us. He decides who gets honored and who doesn't, both here and in eternity: "Riches and honor come from you alone" (1 Chronicles 29:12).

Remember the song "He's Got the Whole World in His Hands"? Those words are still true. Isn't it good to know that God is in complete control of our lives?

☼ Hold That Thought ☼

Thank God today that your life and your future
are in good hands—His!

What the Future Holds

Jesus promises:

"See, I am coming soon, and my reward is with me,
to repay all according to their deeds....
Yes, I am coming soon!" Amen! Come, Lord Jesus!
Revelation 22:12, 20

Jesus is coming soon! Are you loving Him with all your heart? Are you loving others? Are you ready? He wants so much for you to experience every reward possible, but it all depends on how you live your life now.

Maybe you don't feel ready yet. Don't lose hope! God will help you: "Now may the God of peace make you holy in every way, and may your whole spirit and soul and body be kept blameless until that day when our Lord Jesus Christ comes again. God, who calls you, is faithful; he will do this" (1 Thessalonians 5:23–24).

Did you catch that? God is faithful, and He will make you holy in every way. Let Him help you. Trust Him. Believe that He has power enough to make you like His Son. Believe it and live it, and the reward will be yours!

☼ Hold That Thought ☼

You're doing great! You're on the road to the rewards that God will give you in the end. He won't let you miss out! Thank God for this today. And keep reaching forward, reaching up, reaching out. Let Jesus and the whole world know that you belong to Him, you serve Him, and your reward—today and in heaven—is with Him. Come, Lord Jesus!

Begin an Eternal
Adventure

A LIFE GOD REWARDS™ GUYS ONLY

Speaks specifically to developing young men, helping them live their lives to make a difference forever.
ISBN 1-59052-096-3

A LIFE GOD REWARDS™ GUYS 90 DAY CHALLENGE

More than just a devotional, this is a personalized challenge to find out how to please God in everything you do today.
ISBN 1-59052-098-X

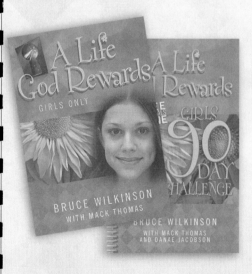

A LIFE GOD REWARDS™ GIRLS ONLY

A revolutionary message presented in a captivating package for girls 9–12 as they begin to form their feminine identity.
ISBN 1-59052-097-1

A LIFE GOD REWARDS™ GIRLS 90 DAY CHALLENGE

More than just a devotional, this is a personalized challenge to find out how to please God in everything you do today.
ISBN 1-59052-099-8

God Rewards His Kids

A LIFE GOD REWARDS™ FOR KIDS

Early readers can learn for themselves the important biblical concept of storing up treasure in heaven. Age-appropriate text with fun cartoon illustrations.

ISBN 1-59052-095-5

A LIFE GOD REWARDS™ FOR LITTLE ONES

An eye-catching board book introduces preschoolers to a loving heavenly Father who longs to reward them in the biggest way possible.

ISBN 1-59052-094-7

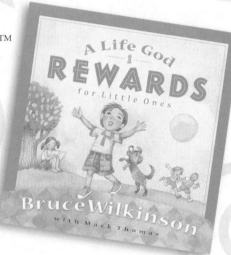

A Teen Shares Fresh Perspectives on Life For Everyone Who Is Still Learning

"...captures the joys and challenges of her generation."
BRUCE WILKINSON, author of the *New York Times* bestseller *The Prayer of Jabez for Teens*

things
I've
learned
lately

DANAE
JACOBSON

Teenager Danae Jacobson, an exciting new voice in young adult publishing, offers insights and asks questions gleaned from a perceptive and refreshingly simple view of the world around her. In a debut book, *Things I've Learned Lately,* her short essays on the life lessons she's experienced discuss everything from love and relationships to the meaning of seasons and of death. Chapters include "Midnight Laughing Cleanses You," "There Is a Time for Everything," and "The Stars Shine Brighter When There Is No Moon." Danae explores simple truths such as, "Forgiving someone is proof of your love," and, "Coincidences are really 'God-things,'" offering an honest, hopeful approach to young people who, like herself, are striving to match the challenges of life with a firm faith.

ISBN 1-57673-951-1

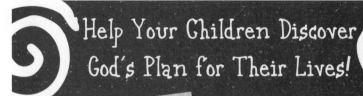

Help Your Children Discover God's Plan for Their Lives!

Secrets of the Vine™ for Kids
1-4003-0053-3

SECRETS
of
THE VINE™
for Kids

BRUCE
WILKINSON

The Prayer of Jabez™ for Kids
0-8499-7944-7

Also Available (not pictured)

The Prayer of Jabez for Little Ones
0-8499-7943-9
The Prayer of Jabez Devotions for Kids
0-8499-7945-5
The Prayer of Jabez for Young Hearts
0-8499-7932-3
The Prayer of Jabez for Kids:
A Praise & Worship Experience (CD)
1-4003-0065-7
The Prayer of Jabez for Kids:
A Praise & Worship Experience (Cass)
1-4003-0064-9
The Prayer of Jabez for Young Hearts (Cass)
1-4003-0066-5
Secrets of the Vine for Young Hearts
1-4003-0055-X
Secrets of the Vine Devotions for Kids
1-4003-0054-1

The Prayer of Jabez for
Young Hearts (CD)
1-4003-0067-3

Secrets of the Vine for Little Ones
1-4003-0052-5

Tommy NELSON

www.tommynelson.com